MW01047056

CALLING ALL SUBS

"*SUB*servient", "*SUB*sidiary", "*SUB*standard", "*SUB*ordinant" —these are only a few of the terms that aptly describe the general sentiment towards Substitute Teachers. As many would attest, it is an unfortunate state of affairs that this attitude toward substitute teachers is not only shared on the part of students, but full-time faculty all the same. Moreover, one may argue that the first word used to describe this essential occupation, "substitute," carries with it a certain level of contempt, and thereby bears some responsibility for the stigma associated with this most necessary aspect of grade school education.

-*Carl Vann, Jr.*

Melvilyn Scott

Infinity Publications, LLC.
Vanderbilt Media House, LLC.
999 Waterside Drive
Suite 110
Norfolk, VA 23510
(804)286-6567

www.vanderbiltmediahouse.net
Library of Congress Control Number: 2022905831
ISBN-13 : 978-1-953096-24-1
First Edition : October 2022
10 9 8 7 6 5 4 3 2 1
This book was printed in the United States
Book cover illustrated by Leena Shariq
Interior illustrations by students: Deanna and Deonna Johnson
Scriptures marked KJV are taken from the King James Version and NKJV from the New Kings James Version

Table of Contents

Melvilyn Scott

Foreword

With the most recent horrific events that have taken place.

We want to make sure our kids are in a safe space.

Shots ring out in school shootings and our kids hit the floor.

We are pleading and begging please no more.

VA Tech, Sandy Hook, Marjory Stoneman,

Robb Elementary, and so many to name.

We have to stop this violence…this is no game.

We stand in unison to protect our future and be the buffer.

We are crying out for change so that no one else has to suffer.

~Of the hearts and minds of people who care~

CALLING ALL SUBS

Dedication

Dedicated to Tony, my loving husband and best friend;

my daughter Nakesha;

my sons, Solomon and Malachi;

my granddaughters, Akira and Areana;

my great grandson, Ky'ere;

and my Sunday School class.

They have always supported me in every endeavor

that I have ever embarked on!

No matter how serious or silly.

Know that I love all of you!

Special thanks to Carl Vann, Sr., Carl Vann, Jr., & Lovie Harris

Melvilyn Scott

Introduction

This book is for all the substitute or guest teachers who go into the trenches to work in the public school system. Years ago, I was once a substitute teacher, so I feel your pain, I empathize, sympathize and I am asking you why you continue to do it?!

This pandemic which our country has faced has not made it any easier. It has got to be more than for a paycheck...Right? I started to title the book, "Stories You Would Not Believe...From Inside of The Public School System," instead "Calling All Subs" sounded so much better since these are just a few stories of me being a substitute teacher. Some of us believe that we can make a difference, even if it is no more than to touch the life of one child at a time who is our future.

I wrote this book because I had a naïve outsider's view of our public school system and our children, to be honest and transparent. Now, the disclaimer is that every school is not the same. Every school system, teacher, janitor, lunch lady or bus monitor is not the same. But if there is a problem in one school, it is one problem too many, because our children are being impacted. I was impacted. So, what do we do? Do we run? Do we stand?!

Umm, maybe we stand...wayyyyy back because I'm too old to run...Well, I want to thank you for taking this journey with me in advance... As you will see I like to use a lot of...ellipses in my writing. Please don't be annoyed, I am not a professional writer, excuse any errors...I'm just someone trying to tell a few funny stories and help make someone's day!

This Is My Journey...Let's Travel Together
"Let me just give you a brief summary on this journey."

That was the question I kept asking myself... Well, being transparent, I will tell you why I wanted to become a substitute teacher... I needed a job, and I was qualified. I had a wonderful job, but it ended, due to no fault of my own and I was left without that major source of income. Unemployment is nice, but... oh yeah there is always a but...Like I was saying, I was receiving unemployment, but it doesn't last forever, and it is a percentage of what you actually used to make.

Nevertheless, I was grateful for the weekly unemployment checks, but I *had* to work., I am not the type of person who just sits around doing nothing. That is not in my family's DNA, and *anyway* I am an educated woman. Who wouldn't want to hire me? Oh yeah, if you don't hear it coming off the page you should...yeah that's the sound of being overly confident! Yeah, I have THREE degrees and I am working on my FOURTH! Oh yeah, I am OVER qualified! Substitute teaching will be a piece of cake. I already teach at the college level, so hard could it be? Oh yeah, the confidence is just oozing off the page and flowing down the stream of haughtiness.

For those of you who can't stop snarling at the page as you read it, or for those of you who just can't stop laughing, give me a moment, there is more!

As I applied to become a substitute teacher, I said to myself and even out loud..."How hard can it be?" I'll just do this until something else comes along. I can do this…Oh yeah, I can do this!

Note to self:

I can do this!

A cheerful heart is good medicine, but a broken spirit saps a person's strength.-**Proverbs 17:22 NKJV**
Trust and believe that most substitutes
have cheerful hearts and are strong!

So, Who Would Want to Be a Substitute Teacher?
"What was my motivation for becoming a substitute teacher...and what may become yours?"

And I did, but boy was I in for a rude awakening! As you continue to read you will find that I will be using avatars to express how I was feeling doing some of my funny, sad, and joyful times I had as a substitute teacher. I have created my own personal avatars to express how I was feeling on those days I came home speechless. Now I don't know how long this book will be around, but I know with today's technology a lot more is said with avatars than with words. For those of you who are out of the technology loop, an avatar is an image which says what you are trying to say with a picture, gesture, or sign.

A picture is worth a thousand words, and let me tell you, there were some days when I would just text my husband an avatar and he would know exactly what type of day I was having! Some of those pictures expressed my feelings, my frustrations better than I ever could with words, and I was keeping it clean!

Oh yeah, emojis and avatars became my best friends. They understood me! They felt my pain. They always could tell my story!

CALLING ALL SUBS

Thank you, emojis and avatars. What would I have done without you? LOL (for those you who don't quite get this new shorthand *LOL* means laugh out loud, not lots of love or lose it loser). So, throughout the book, you will see my own personal avatars (or shall I say an attempt to draw an avatar). I can't afford to pay for the rights to use those wonderful characters used in text messages on and your phones! Nevertheless, I believe you will get the point. And while I am at it… I would just like to acknowledge my Sunday school class.

When I started on my journey as a substitute teacher, they would not laugh at me but try to help me understand what was going on while I was teaching.

Some Sundays they would be praying for me! They tried to "school me" on school. I must admit that they were a tremendous help! So, when I decided to write a book about my experiences two wonderful young ladies agreed to help me illustrate this book and as you will see that they did an excellent job and I just want to thank them… Now back to the story .

So back to why anyone would want to become a substitute teacher. Well, most of my substitute teacher colleagues needed the money. Sad but true. In today's economy you do what you have to do and make it work (legally speaking).

It is an honest living; you feel like you have an opportunity to make a difference in the lives of our future and you go for it! In most states (yes, I did my research), you must have some college education to be deemed worthy of being a substitute teacher in the public-school system. However, in some states (which I will not mention) you do not have to have anything more than a high school diploma a GED and just be breathing. You know what... I literally wrote this before I did any true research with hopes that I had made a mistake in my assumptions ...but unfortunately what I wrote was accurate and true. What can I say?

Today's public school systems need a lot of help and substitute teachers help fill the gap. But is this job the one for you? Notice I use the word job and not career, because there is a difference. Some substitute teachers and long-term teachers are looking for those schools who can help them pay off their student loans ...now let's not get into that...But I must ask...will you help fill the gap? I thought this employment choice was the one for me...at least temporarily. Oh, my goodness...was I in for a treat!

Note to self:

Research on google has shown that some cities pay more than others and require more education, so it's worth applying to more than one city to work as a substitute. Google is my friend. You can find almost anything on google.

CALLING ALL SUBS

I have applied...Hire Me...Train Me...I Can Do This!

"Yea mandatory and application and hiring process. This will give you some insight and understanding of my journey."

S o now what? I have submitted my application to become a substitute teacher, and I am anticipating that wonderful phone call. Yes, Mrs. Educated, we saw your application and had to call you immediately. We just must have you come to work for us. We know that you are overqualified but would you do us the honor of coming to work for us and help us out. We know you may not be with us long, but please come and help us out for just a little bit.

Well, I really didn't think that they would say all of that. I know better for in Proverbs 16:18, *Pride goes before destruction, And a haughty spirit before a fall.*(NKJ)

I knew that I was qualified, and I really needed a job. So, I did expect to get some type of notification in a timely manner about my glowing application and resume. Days went by, weeks went by, months went by, and I didn't hear anything back at all, except that they had received my application. What type of mess is this? Don't they know who I am? What type of establishment is this anyway? Do I really want to work for them if this is how they treat me in the beginning? Ummm yeah, you need a job, so yeah, you will work with them as soon as you get that call.

No Call? Well, time went by, and no call came. I am feeling really rejected at this point. As much education, and debt that I am in, you mean to tell me that I can't even get a substitute teaching job. Are you serious? Do you know who long and complicated that application was? What do you need all that stuff for anyway? Sheesh! They don't deserve me; they don't know that it's their loss that they have not called me…Wait for it…Wait for it…Are you serious? I have been offered a job through an email??

No not a job but an opportunity for a job. What? Come in for an orientation in two days and bring all your documents *to try to* become a substitute teacher. Yes, I said *try to* become.

7

WHAT? This packet is 4 billion pages long and they want 10 additional pages of information. ARE YOU SERIOUS? Hold on…I have to pay for my own background check…what if I don't get the job, do I get my money back?! Lord have mercy! I need a job. Lord…Thank you for the opportunity. Forgive me for my ungratefulness. I have faith that you will take care of me.

Note to self:

For I say, through the grace given unto me, to every man that is among you, not to think of himself more highly than he ought to think; but to think soberly, according as God hath dealt to every man the measure of faith. **(Romans 12:3 KJV)**

"Thank you, Lord, for the reminder…"

Orientation day...Remember I said that I was an educated individual. As a matter of fact, I am an overly confident, educated individual. Well even educated people don't follow directions or read. In those 10 trillion pages of instructions, I neglected to read (*because I know everything*), that I had to take two tests online, have an unofficial transcript, and have paid for my background check before even attending the orientation. Yes, I think you need for me to write that again so that you can get the full effect...

In addition, the office where you have to pay for the background check is halfway across town in the opposite direction from where the orientation is located. *ARE YOU SERIOUS!* Oh my God! So needless to say, the morning of, I am on the computer, because that is what overly confident educated people do; they wait to the last minute to get all of their documents together for a job, and guess what? You have to be there in 2 hours and you have 3 hours' worth of things to get done before you go, such as take two mandatory quizzes on identifying abuse. Yep, you gotta get it done before you go to this orientation. *WHAT?* They are each an hour long! So, who do you blame...educated person, if you miss out on your chance to get this job?...You cannot blame anyone but yourself. All of this to become a substitute teacher. WOW, it's more to this than I thought. *I am very impressed!*

The Orientation…

I am no longer impressed. Orientation is a PowerPoint Presentation and a collection of all of the papers that you asked me to bring. What? Are you **serious**? Lord help me…as I look around, I am thinking…**seriously**! I am dressed professionally and expecting this room to be filled with the same, but these people shall say, don't meet *my* requirements…*Well*, just put it this way…what I was expecting is not what I saw. Half of the people did not have all of the paperwork required (as expressed in the 500 billion-ka-trillion-page packet…trees just lost their lives for nothing!) Some people were late, uh…me included because I was still trying to get all of that paperwork together (*don't judge me, lol.*) But I would never enter into a session being more than 15 minutes late. Um again…don't judge me. Remember, I need a job. Should I mention that there were others who came in an hour late and still were able to go through the orientation? Oh my goodness really! It's none of my business but really...Maybe they called ahead and had a valid reason for showing up late… NOT… Oh yeah, I couldn't help ear hustling (*you know listening in on their conversation*), they were just late and still didn't have all of their required paperwork. Again, I am no longer impressed. They don't know who I am from a hill of beans. I could have sent someone to come in my place to do all of this! Really! Lord help me change my attitude. Don't judge me!…Since the rewriting of this book I have discovered that orientation is very different. Maybe they knew that this book was coming out…nevertheless as they would say… this is how it was then.

Orientation is over. Is that it? Collect my paperwork and I wait on another email. What about training. This PowerPoint cannot be all that I get today. I am going to work with children, and I am not given any type of T-R-A-I-N-I-N-G. Whoa. That's it? OK, so I am *really* no longer impressed. So now I just wait?? While writing this book, any decent credible writer does some research. I am new to this writing thing, but I knew I at least should answer some of my own questions about substitute teaching in other states.

There is a website which you can log on to and research the qualifications to become a substitute teacher in every state. Again, some requirements are very minimal, however some do offer training. But this was not my case. Nevertheless, we move on. Now it is the waiting game. I sit by the computer and wait on my email. A big sigh and I wait. Now keep in mind I am a new substitute teacher. By no means do I know everything about substitute teaching in all of our wonderful states, I am speaking of my own personal experiences, and honestly, I find a lot of humor and sometimes sadness in what I experienced, and I want you to continue the journey with me!

The email arrives. Oh my! I have been approved to teach; I mean substitute…in ever literal sense of the word (you will understand later what I mean)! I feel important, I feel valued, I feel needed, *I have a job*…or do I? Now I have to watch a series of videos and figure out how to let people know I want to work. Oh my…that's how it works. Everything is automated. I can wait and receive a phone call in the morning and just be ready to jump up and rush to a school, or I can log in online and search for a job and try to be the first to snag it before someone else does at that school.

Oh my…it's work to get work.

Wait for it…Wait for it…Whoop whoop! Thank you Lord!

I snagged my first job!

Note to self:

Things are looking up, you have a job, and you are going to make a difference in the lives of our future!

"Be careful for nothing; but in everything by prayer and supplication with thanksgiving let your requests be made known unto God." Proverbs 4:6 (KJV)

CALLING ALL SUBS

My First Day

"My first day as a substitute teacher...the journey begins. Thank you for joining me."

O h my, I am so excited. I chose a charter school! Yes, I chose the school I wanted to go to. My choice! I feel empowered! The only downfall is that I am working the second half of the day! I know this school. I have seen this school from the outside and have heard good things about this school. It is going to be a breeze. I am working with first graders. Yes, this was my choice. How bad can it be? What is the phrase that our youth use today? Oh yeah… "*I got this!"*

I teach Sunday School to middle school students and guess what I *sometimes* substitute for the first graders...Oh yeah, I think I am ready!

Meeting the Teacher. Oh yeah, I'm early, because that is what I do! I get to meet the teacher because she hasn't left yet and she's not happy that they make her take a half a day…Well I'm happy because it gives me a chance to earn some money. She gives me her plans, wishes me well, and leaves. "*I got this.*" Ummm, why is she wishing me well?

Time to meet our future. Oh yeah, I got this! So far so good. As I walk into the cafeteria to gather my class (aww that sounds so sweet…my class), I see them nicely lined up against the wall like nice little angels. Yes, yes, and yes…

Pump the breaks…Ummm I am quickly told that this is not the class I am substituting for…my class is the table where they are bouncing from chair-to-chair throwing food at each other and the lunch monitor is telling three of them to clean up their mess...(yeah there is milk and food on the floor under the entire table). Really, this is my class? No wonder the teacher wished me well! I don't believe in wishes…she should have been praying for me. I take a breath and I know I can do this. They had so much cleaning up to do, we were the last class to leave the lunchroom.

I then worked to get them lined up while they ask me four bazillion questions. *Are you the taking Mrs. X's class? Is she sick? Is she coming back? What's your name again? Where did you come from? You're tall! Is that your real hair?* Johnny kicked me so he can't have recess. Yadda, Yadda, Yadda, Yadda…

I finally tuned them out, that's when the lunch lady came over and screamed something at them then they fall in line, and I walk them to the classroom. After we got to the classroom, one by one they began whining, then screaming, "*I have to go to the bathroom!*" Really? I can't believe this. We just barely made it to the classroom. It's not on the lesson plan…LOL! I am going to lay down the law and we are going to have a great day! Umm, why are they crying? Why are they chasing each other around the room and not listening to me? Why are you holding your crotch little man and bouncing up and down...oh that's right you have to go to the bathroom! Wait a minute...this is not how it's supposed to be. Did that child just say, shut up?

Oh my... As I sit here and write about this first day, all I can do is laugh! You may not be laughing but that's OK because I am. This is therapeutic for me! Oh my, I was in a state of shock. What have I gotten myself into? Oh my... the runny noses, the language, the lack of language, the hitting, the pushing, the glares, the frowned faces, the rolling around on the floor, and the tantrums!

Oh NO! He's under the table and I can't get to him! I'm too old for this...Please come from under the table Little Johnny or whatever your name is.... Lord please don't let someone come in here right now! Ahhhhh the screaming! Oh, the whining...Please stop crying! *Ewww*, please get your snotty hands off of my pants! Ladies and gentlemen, this is not your normal snot...*Ewww*, I've seen snot before, but I don't think this goo is going to come off my pants... I think it's burning a hole in them... I'll never be able to wear these pants again. I may have to call the hazmat team to dispose of them...

THE PANTS ARE RUINED...

16

Oh Lord! What do I do? Suck it up and get control of this situation soldier. Take a deep breath. Breathe, breathe...Ok, I've got it! I'll turned the lights off and that will get their attention. ....Wait for it...Wait for it...but that didn't help. Now they are screaming and hollering because they are afraid. OMG! Gain control...scream at the top of your lungs to get their attention and calm them down. Please don't let anyone peek in the window or visit this room. They'll remove me immediately. Lord, help your daughter...Just close your eyes and pray for a moment...

No, you can't close your eyes gurl, you've got to watch the kids. Pray with your eyes open... Lord please help me! Inhale...exhale...inhale, exhale...Ummm what are they doing? It just got quiet all of a sudden, that can't be good, can it? They are all in a corner doing something...but what? One child has an iPad out and they are mesmerized.

Where did she get that answer to my prayer? Bend down

and ask Little Johnny who just wiped his hands on my pants *again* *Ewww* to show me where the iPads are! He smiles and grabs my hand to lead me to them *Ewww* his hands are sticky…. Parents, please send hand sanitizer to school for your children.

Note to myself:

Bring your large bottle of sanitizer with you, that little bottle hanging off your purse is not enough!

He leads me to a cabinet and.... praise God...there is enough for every child! Hallelujah! Thank you, Father God! Maybe now I can get back on track and try to get some of these things done on the lesson plan left by the teacher. Ummm...Let's talk about these Teacher's/Lesson Plans.

Teacher's Plans. Teacher's plans are supposed to be outlines of what the actual teacher would be doing that day. So, since the teacher is not there, we are to carry on the class as usual. Notice I put a "we" there...So you are a substitute with me... Yes, you have to take this journey with me to get the full effect! So why is it that they use acronyms and alien shorthand to communicate to a substitute teacher who is unfamiliar with this foreign language what they want us to do? Also...why in the world would a teacher leave us work to do that they can't even get their students to do. Is this a set up for failure? Teacher... I am raising my hand (visualize me raising my hand). If you couldn't get Little Johnny to figure out the water cycle...why is this now our *task and responsibility?* You don't know me like that....to want to torture me! I'm a nice person, really, I am, you can ask anybody.

Why won't you warn me about the special children in your class who always cause problems? Please tell me why? Can you give me some type of warning! A wink, two stars, a thumbs up, a thumbs down? No that would be toooo easy...you just write in your plans if I need help go to the next room or call the office/security and give me a stack of referrals. A stack of referrals for first grade...*SERIOUSLY!* Why can't you move those wonderful children to another class for the day that you are out! I have one question. Do your subs ever return? *Hmmm, something to think about...*

This is a true story and I have no need to lie....On one assignment I was at this particular school with slightly older scholars and as the nice substitute teacher I am, I stood at the door and greeted all the students who came in by saying good morning. I also was smiling and saying good morning to those in the hallway...however, not one individual said good morning. Not one! The teacher across the hall even looked at me funny and didn't even speak. They were looking at me like I was crazy. I kept smiling and greeting each one as they entered the class, but I was honestly thinking to myself manners are free. It cost you nothing to say good morning, and just before the bell rang one student came in and sat down in a chair and said, "Oh y'all have a sub ...y'all ain't gonna do no work" then got up and left the class. I kid you not...Then the bell rung and I closed the door and said good morning again, and began to take attendance when lo and behold **four** students walked in. Not one, not two, not three but four!

One student had a bag of chips and a drink and slid down

in a chair in front of me and began to crunch and slurp. Now remember, I was trying to take attendance before they walked in. So, they have interrupted attendance and now he is eating in front of me. Now there is supposed to be no food or drinks allowed in the class and the signs are posted. (*Do you see the signs? Well, if you don't I guess he didn't either*). So, do I choose to fight this battle, or do I let it go, plus he is already late. So, I begin to introduce myself and before I could finish my name, my chip chomper says, "I always get in trouble when we have a sub. The last time I got suspended." (Can you see the expression on my face? Just try to imagine.) OK, so now what? Well, needless to say…as much as I tried redirection, including him into the class projects, and then just ignoring him all together, he still was disruptive and had to be removed from the class with two other students. Ladies and gentlemen and all those who are reading this, Lord knows I tried to work with this young person. I kept saying to myself *"provoke not your children to anger, lest they be discouraged,"* Colossians 3:21. Then immediately, *Spare the rod and Spoil the child* crossed all of that out! Wait, wait, wait, this is not my child, and I cannot put my hands on him! Whew… bring it back in!

So, my question is **Why** wasn't he removed from the class. Is that asking too much? He is a known substitute antagonist! He has a proven track record for traumatizing subs.

Thanks a lot! Now on the other hand, when I have had the opportunity to meet with some of the teachers before they take leave, they do name the possible overly chatty, rather rambunctious, won't stay in their seat, disrespectful and combative students. Some have even said,

"Thank you for subbing for me today, and I have removed, Little Won't Stay in his Seat, Chatty Kathy, and Ben the Bully, out of the class for you today because you just don't need that headache!"

WOW, I just love that! Wow what a great teacher, a real human being with passion and consideration! I just want to hug you right now! I know that you deal with this every day and I am just the sub and I would have to deal with it for just one day, but it does the rest of the class a disservice if I have to figure out how to deal with these challenging students, as I work through the lesson plans. I do not have a sense of entitlement, but I would just like some warning and common courtesy...No. Let's just call it fair and justice for the substitutes. Now back to these lesson plans...Please give us enough class work to make it through the day for the students.

You know that some of your students work faster than others, and some of them you never leave enough work for! Now what do I do? I have no clue, they are finished, even though they rushed through it and it is very sloppy. You and I both know that they are not going to go back and redo it neatly, this is how they turn in all of their work, and I see proof of it in those bins that you have which is where the homework is placed. Yeah, there is a stack of papers to be graded with the same sloppy work. Those of you taking this journey with me, I am not talking about elementary school scholars. I am talking about young adults.

Note to self:

It's not that bad, or is it? I'll just be like the Little Engine That Could... I think I can, I think I can, I think I can...you're working and you're teaching and that is your passion... I think I can, I think can, I think I can...I think I will, I think I will look for another school and another grade.

CALLING ALL SUBS

Hazard Pay
"Uh, yeah, this section is very interesting.
I am giving you more warning than anyone gave me!"

The *Reality of it All*. Now that I have been doing this for a while, yeah, I am a pro all of a month. So, let me just share with you that I am an older and more mature person with graciously incoming gray hair. Some of the young scholars have even called me old lady. Well, trust me after some of these incidents I did begin to really feel old because when I was growing up, some of these experience…no I will say none of these incidents would have ever taken place. We had respect for all adults and after these experiences I was left completely dumbfounded and appalled at some of the youth. We had respect for adults. Some of them haven't had any old-fashioned discipline…if you know what I mean! Somebody is going to say something about that last line right there. But I wrote it, it made the edits, and I am not taking it out! I remember an old Andy Griffith episode where he asked a father if he wanted to use his old woodshed to deal with his spoiled son! Oh, my goodness, where are the old woodsheds from long ago??? You must see this episode…

https://www.youtube.com/watch?v=wKBnPPkCasY.

However, I must admit…some, not all of these young people are very, very, very disrespectful. My goodness. Some of these young people are so **DISREPECTFUL** and have a sense of entitlement.

Should I go on?...and this is what they say in ELEMENTARY SCHOOL! So how do you motivate students with these types of attitudes as a SUBSTITUTE TEACHER?

Lord, help the teachers who report every day to deal with these young minds. Yeah, I know, you could say, well your just there for a day. Why make them do anything. Well, let me tell you... you cannot make these students do anything! They have their own minds, their own strong wills, and their own support and sometimes it is not just the parents but the schools. So, because the teacher has left plans and assignments it is my job as a substitute teacher to try to get all of them, not some of them, to do their work. I agreed to substitute for the entire class, including the Chatty Cathy, Little Johnnie, and Aaron the Antagonist. I will do my best to get it done because it is what I signed up for! Call it my ethical responsibility because it is my job... Nevertheless, we are going to keep on pressing on! If you were never warned. Now you are warned our journey is not quite over.

THIS IS A WARNING!

Note to self:

**Let us not become weary in doing good, for at the proper time
we will reap a harvest if we do not give up.**

CALLING ALL SUBS

YOU SHOULD HAVE TOLD ME! Yes, substitutes should be told about the dynamics of the class they sign up for. One tooo many times, I thought I was taking a 1ˢᵗ grade class only to be told that it was 3ʳᵈ grade. In some cases, there is a resource teacher who helps out during the day. However, they come and go and I think they are playing games, just like the students when the substitutes come as well.

True Story… I was in a middle school and I began to take attendance when I noticed one student talking while I was trying to take attendance. I thought she was being very disrespectful, so I said, "Good morning" and she rolled her eyes at me...Let us pause right there! For those of you who need a visual, eyerolling is an art for some young people and they do it well. Her eye rolling showed skill. She looked at me, made eye contact, closed her eyes and they you could see the insides of her eyes move from one side of her face to the other (now this is all done while she is looking at me with her eyes closed)…then she opens her eyes and physically turns her head away from me in the opposite direction. In one smooth motion, she then turns her upper body in direct alignment with her head to make sure none of her body was facing me. NOW that takes skill. The students just burst out laughing! Then one of the students said,

"Oh, she's not a student. She's the aide for this class that's why she's ignoring you."

I shook my head and said 'hello' again. She turned her entire desk around to make sure she was not facing me and continued to talk with the other students. Now when she walked in she did not introduce herself, she did not say good morning, but sat down and started chatting with the other students, I kid you not… she blended in with the students and made no attempt during the class to help me during the class. As a matter of fact, when one of the students asked her why she wasn't a substitute, she said ...and I quote as she turned her head to look at me…her voice elevated and she said... *"I would never be a substitute teacher; they don't make enough."* Then she looked at me and rolled her eyes…again!

Boy oh boy! Thank God for Jesus. Of course, the rest of the class period was barely controllable because all she did was talk with the students and distract them from their lessons. So, I ask you...do I write a note to the regular teacher and inform her about the lack of assistance, or do I suck it up and keep it moving (stop being a tattle tale)… Well, I was invited to have lunch with a few teachers, and I learned it was best to just suck it up and keep it moving. Trust and believe, I have had wonderful experiences with other aides, resource teachers and paraprofessionals but this situation is one for the record books. Hey, not only is it good for the record books but I have found it worthy of this book. I pray she reads this and remembers who she is... Am I being a Petty Betty right now!? No, because this young lady needs to understand that she never knows who is in the classroom to observe. This is a teachable moment! I really don't think she cares about the students. She was more concerned about being their friend versus working to help them understand their lesson. What a wow moment...but trust me there is more to come!

You should have warned me...Teachers you should have warned me that these students can sometimes be violent and attack other students as well as faculty and staff. That was not provided when the assignment was posted. You should have told me that I would be in the class of 23 students alone and I had several on the autism spectrum. Why is that important? Because these children and gifted, talented, and don't always warm up to new people or like change. Especially if it is thrown on them at the last minute without warning. You should have told me that I signed up for a 2nd grade class, but it is actually a 3rd grade class with students old enough to be in high school. You should have told me!

Melvilyn Scott

Where is my hazard pay!?

These students are as big as I am, as tall as I am and to be honest….know more than I know when it comes to the school and the expectation….What about my hazard pay? Breaking up fights was not in the lesson plan. Being kicked, spit on and accosted, was not listed in the job description. Did I miss something in orientation? Let me go back to that day...Uhhh, nothing in the Power Point about having to take a self-defense class to feel safe. Is hip checking a loudmouth, arrogant, misguided student allowed? Yeah, I like basketball for my basketball friends out there! You should have warned me. Nobody warned me! SMH (I am shaking my head so much that sometimes it looked like I was watching a tennis match). Nobody warned me! The day has got to get better. Maybe at lunch.

Note to self:

The Lord will fight for you; you need only to be still.
Exodus 14:14 (KJV)

31

Melvilyn Scott

Lunch?? What's That?
"Depending how old you are...
This might mean something different today."

OK it's lunch time…Now depending on the school …lunch can be something very different for a substitute at each school. Remember, in one school I was invited to have lunch with other faculty in their teacher's lounge. I have also been told that I can sit in the classroom and eat lunch, or it can be a special time to bond with the young minds of the future or ***a time to change your assignment during your break so that you don't have to return tomorrow***! Yes, lunch at school is different. You can be in a jungle or in paradise.

During my tours of these academic institutions, I have discovered several things…the volume in the lunchrooms is deafening! The students rush, push, and shove in the line to get food that they don't end up eating but start playing with. In addition, there is one disturbing trend I have identified with our younger scholars in elementary schools… some parents just send their kids to school with money and never expect any change. Little Johnnie's ice cream habit cost more than the lunch each day at $5.00 a week. What is even more confusing is that he's not eating the lunch or ice cream.

One too many days …what was on their lunch trays ended in someone's hair, on someone's shirt, on someone's shoes, or in someone's nose, '*Ewww.*'

Yeah, lunch was a great adventure at each school. Noise, noise, and more noise… It was deafening. I thought it was lunch time. Time to eat, not scream and yell at each other. Oh my, I don't want to see your food! People, please chew with your mouth's closed. Please close your mouths…food flying out of your mouth is not attractive or cute even for a first grader and it is worse for a middle or high schooler. Let us not talk about high school. What world do these young people come from? Oh, my goodness, if I knew I was going to write a book, I would have taken more detailed notes. Such things I can remember is:

- *They push each other in line to get lunch …then they don't even eat it!*

- *They play with their food and then complain later that they are hungry!*

- *There is always one person who tries to sneak part of their lunch back to the classroom.*

- *There is always someone who has to try to cut the line and cause a problem. Oh yeah cutting someone is when you get in the line in front of other people instead of getting in the back of the line.*

So, during this special time of day, I asked myself …

What is lunch?

Lots of
Unruly
Noisy
Children
Hollering

So, let's never forget that's what lunch means. I don't know how the kids do it, but some time's I do understand why they throw their food around; they don't think of it as food but something to play with. Lunch, my how the time does fly during this brief period which is supposed to be your time. Now it's time to go and get our future leaders so that the day can continue.

CALLING ALL SUBS

Resource and Recess
"The two R's should stand for Rest and Rescue"

Resource and Recess are special times for our young scholars. It is a time to enjoy the arts, go to gym or go outside and burn off some energy. Resource and Recess are the R & R's for substitute teachers.

Resource in schools today provides our young scholars an opportunity to become enlightened with ART, MUSIC, and other exploratory classes. It is great and it gives our young scholars to be exposed to things other than reading, writing, science, and social studies. On many occasions, it is built into a day's student schedule and is substituted for recess.

Recess in the 21st century is now something new and not every day. As mentioned earlier, it alternates with RESOURCE days and guess what...you can have recess in the classroom. ***What?*** Even on a sunny day, when it is beautiful outside? Most of the students would rather just sit in front on an iPad. Yes, these little tablets have captured the hearts of our youth and what I discovered is...no matter what type of parental controls or blocks you have on these tablets....Little Johnny knows how to get around those blocks and go to unapproved websites! And guess what?...They share how they do it so that everyone can do it...Smart little cookies aren't they?

As smart as they are and as wise as they may seem, they are still kids. Some of these kids who like to have recess, play dodge ball, play basketball, jump rope, and just run around outside while chasing each other. Yes, they are still just kids with a lot of energy. If this energy could be harvested, it could provide the world with all of the natural power needed to light this entire planet. Going outside to breathe the fresh air… there is nothing like it! The kids love it and truly hate to have to come back inside.

I discovered going to the gym was also one activity the students liked no matter what age group. It was another opportunity for them to be kids. But, you know that there is always a but…There is always one or two and in some instances 10-12 students who misbehave and have to sit out during the fun activities. This is just sad, to have to take away the one thing that they enjoy…but sometimes this helps them to understand that they have to behave in school. If they act like this in school, the question asked is how do they act at home? I heard a young preacher say in a Wednesday night service, "The school didn't make your kids bad or make them the way they are…some of the parents are responsible for their behavior…stop blaming the school for Little Johnny's behavior."

Can I say drop the mic!

Is this true for all children?...NO! Is it true for a lot of children...MAYBE...Is it true for some children YES!

It is so perfectly clear why Little Johnny acts the way he acts when the parents come to the school and want to defend Little Johnny's unacceptable behavior. Or better yet, the parents won't show up for parent teacher conferences, won't return any phone calls, and only come to school to reinstate Little Johnny because he has been suspended.

These are true stories...Little Johnny came to school after being suspended the very next day. He was sitting in his chair like the "angel" we all know he could be first thing in the morning after breakfast. When I asked him why he was back so soon, he said he did not want to be home alone all day and that he never told his mother he was suspended. I am really confused...*She picked him up from school yesterday before lunch and was told he was suspended*...What is really going on? Of course, he was removed from the class and she was called again and said nothing. He was in fact suspended for not one but three days and the mother did not help. Sometimes we can get some insight as to why these young people act the way they act.

These same parents cuss, yes cuss, not curse, but **CUSS** teachers out when their children cannot go on field trips because the child does not know how to act. It is a sad commentary when so much of this holds true. But as stated before, there is always a but...There are those parents who can't be as involved as they want to be. They do their best to support the teachers in their efforts to teach their children. There are also parents who come to visit the school and have lunch with their children when possible. Some parents do understand that their children are a handful and provide support from a distance to help make a teacher's day easier. Yes, there are a lot of caring parents who want the best for their children and work hand in hand with teachers and administrators to get it done. I am a witness and I have seen it with my own two-four eyes (oh yeah, I wear glasses). I need all the help I can get to see what's going on in the classroom.

Nevertheless, we must move on.

CALLING ALL SUBS

Note to self:

We have to love these children unconditionally! We never know what's going on and sometimes the love we show them is the only love that they may receive. It could be a smile, a kind word, or a soft touch on the shoulder (now be careful with those touches on the shoulder...I'm just saying. Do those in public for your safety and to acknowledge it in public that we do care). Whew...had to clarify that one! And yes, we must provide discipline and structure. We may be the only disciple that they receive. We discipline them because we do love them. I remember this old episode of 'Family Affair' (I told you I was older...don't judge me) anyway... Jody, the young man in the show had a friend who received a spanking for doing something wrong. Jody nicely told his friend that he never had been spanked and his friend said if your parents don't spank you...then they don't love you. So, Jody began misbehaving to try to get a spanking and his Uncle Bill didn't understand what was going on because being a parent was all new to him. The children were thrust into his care after the unfortunate death of their parents. So, he was finding his way through this new experience himself. Nevertheless, he had a talk with Jody and figured out what was going on...You must watch the clip to understand and have a laugh!

https://www.youtube.com/watch?v=8FVl6c4ln1w

Dismissal...End of the Day
"Now What?"

Time *to go.* OK...the countdown has begun and depending on the school and the grade it can be a whew or it can be an *Oh My God* help me! You have five minutes before this day is officially over, and these students which represent our future will be leaving. Ok let me look at my plans…(It took me some time but I started looking at the end of the day at the beginning of the day so I would know who was doing what at the end of the day). I have a list of students who ride the bus, are walkers, and are picked up.

My eyes scan the room and I try to remember the names of all of these young people as my mind races to figure out if they are going to do what they are supposed to do and help me out or are they going to sneak away into the abyss, and you never see them again! Oh, and be mindful that you are in trouble for not following the protocol. Arghhhhhh!

Ok the first bell rings and the announcements start. OK…look cool calm and in control (this is very important). Yes, always keep the 3-C's in your mind. Being cool, calm, and in control, not Crying, Cursing, or Crashing. You tell them to be quiet so that you can hear the announcements (*but you are really just buying time to get your thoughts together*).

What next? Are they going to call bus riders by bus number, are they going to call car riders, what are they going to do? What do the teacher plans say? Arghhhhhhhhh!...Are you serious right now?... What kind of instructions are these? Take Johnny to Mrs. Jones classroom 203, take Crystal to Room 175, take Devonte to the gym and by the way 5 other students from another teachers' class will be bringing their students to you for dismissal and you have to walk them all downstairs and outside to make sure that they get on the right bus...

THE RIGHT BUS? Really?...I barely know all of their names. I should have gotten some packing tape and just taped their names to their shirts so I could know 'who' who is. Ummm yeah that doesn't work with students who are not in kindergarten. Curses...Ok...I still look cool. Why is that teacher standing in the doorway and glaring at me?

"Excuse me (*she says with an attitude and sarcasm*)... these kids should have been gone by now and you have duty in the hallway!" (WHAT!!! ARE YOU SERIOUS... THAT'S NOT IN MY PLANS FOR TODAY... OK lady with attitude... do you want to take them? You know I am a Substitute...how long did it take for you to get this chaos under control and you want me to know what to do in a day... really and you're teaching our kids?) ARGGGGGH! Take a deep breath and smile or should I turn away and pretend I didn't hear her because the noise is so deafening? Hmmm do I want to come back to this school?

I have a split second to decide how I am going to respond... "EXCUSE ME!"...she yells this time.. Oh no she didn't yell at me in front of these kids! Just as I opened my mouth to respond, one of the young scholars said to me, "Can I hold your hand as we walk out, I know what to do!" Praise the Lord! I took a deep breath and we walked out and the other students followed because for once they were going to do what they were supposed to do! What a relief! Oh my. Do I have any candy in my purse! I should pay this young scholar!

This was a great day! Oh my...I get big smiles, hugs, and I hope you come back from some of these young scholars and it makes it all worth it! A smile, a hug, and I hope you come back, all made it worth it! Wait a minute... was I supposed to hug a child? Did I just break some rule? Oh, my it happened so fast... but nevertheless we move forward, and I am quickly reminded of those are the moments that I reflect on when parents come to the door and snarl at you because you have lost track of time and they wonder what's taking you so long to let their child go home. Honestly, if I knew that they were outside waiting, I would have let your child go early, because they are the main ones causing distractions and being disrespectful. Now I see, it is crystal clear where they get it from. Oh yeah that explains it! Rude parent translates to rude child. Yeah, it makes sense!

What a way to end my day. What a way to end my day! Yes, just the end of one day, but it is not this way every day because every day and every school is different.

Note to self:

"Remember not the former things, nor consider the things of old." Isaiah 43:18 (KJV).

So, I ask all of you in education, what do we do? We should present positive accolades to our children and for those who are believers, we have to go to pray. We don't run we stand! We pray. I want to believe that even if you are not a believer that you understand that there must be a light in us to cast off the darkness which has a strong presence in our public school system. We have got to pray. Everyone does not have the opportunity to send their children to Christian private schools (and they are not perfect either), so we must protect our children with prayer. We also have to remember that if we leave and we are the light that darkness will have complete control. It took me a little over 4 years to write this book and I kept blaming it on procrastination, then came the horrible Coronavirus.

Until March 2020, the Coronavirus showed up and announced that things were about to change. We had no clue we were about to be blindsided. Things would change around the world as we know it and so would teaching. I know for a fact that parents now have a greater appreciation for teachers and if they don't…all I can ask is… How was it trying to teach Little Johnny about the water cycle or how to play the viola? Yeah, Little Johnny or Cute Cathy are not quite the little angels you profess them to be. Some perspectives have changed and as I said before, a greater appreciation for teachers should've been taken to new heights.

I thought when the Lord gave me this book to write it was just for substitute teachers, in all public schools; however, HE politely informed me that this book was for all teachers. It does not matter if they work for public or private schools. I asked the Lord why for all... and HE politely explained that all teachers whether they are long term substitutes, contract, or long-term teachers, they are technically substitute teachers... because a child's first teacher and lifelong teacher is a child's parent(s) and everyone else is really a substitute. All I could say was WOW.

So, after COVID-19, showed up it really taught us about our children... You mean to tell me that you don't remember the Coronavirus which shut the nation down and forced you and children to be home together...yeah that virus which forced parents to really become their children's teachers in every aspect. So here is a shout out to all of those who are already homeschooling their children...because they are looking at the rest of the world going...

This is normal for us...LOL.

Parents, when things go back to being somewhat the way it was with our children going back to school, please consider supporting each and every teacher more than ever before. Please talk to your local congressperson to advocate for better pay for our teachers. Also, please do what you can to stay in constant communication with your child's teacher because I know for a fact that Little Johnny got on your last nerve while he was home with you ALL DAY! He has gotten on your nerves so bad that you just let him watch TV and play video games all day and you don't even try to get him to do any homework. ***Shame on you!*** Little Johnny needs you to help him and help better prepare him for school. Come on now... help us teachers out!

Hence, to all substitutes, I ask you, why do you do what you do? It cannot be for the pay...it must be, from my experience, it is the opportunity to possibly make a positive impact in the lives of our future.

As I pondered and procrastinated when it came to finishing this book, I really had to think about all those in the trenches that teach on a daily basis. Sometimes it is very challenging, but then there are those times when you are constantly reminded that you are doing the right thing for the right reason. By no means does this book reflect all the challenges which are faced in education, nor does it reflect the vast positive experiences that teachers have.

This is just my perspective and my experience which I want to trust and believe will make someone smile, nod their heads in agreement, and give someone a chuckle. Do I consider myself to be a substitute expert…of course not and because I am not, I figured my next book would be titled *"Stories of Substitute Teachers"* and I would incorporate stories from other substitute teachers nationwide, which I know will have you rolling in the aisles.

So be on the lookout for my next book. Thank you for taking the time to read about some of my adventures as a substitute teacher. I would not have given my experiences for anything in this world. I learned a lot, and I have a greater appreciation for all those who do their best to impart knowledge, wisdom, ethical values, righteous morals, and understanding into our children on a daily basis. God bless each and every one of you!

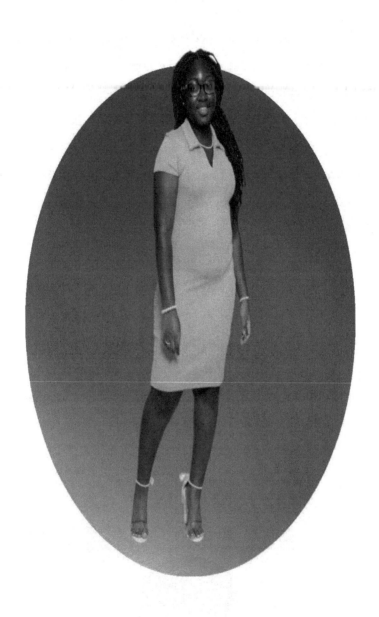

DEANNA JOHNSON
High School Scholar and Illustrator

DEONNA JOHNSON
Currently a Young College Scholar and Illustrator

CALLING ALL SUBS

ILLUSTRATIONS BY DEONNA and DEANNA JOHNSON

Melvilyn Scott

Schools don't have enough short-term teachers to fill in the gaps. School districts in some states are now holding one day online training to get short-term subs, even ones without teaching backgrounds.

NOTES

The expectation of substitute teachers is to accomplish the instructional and classroom management for teachers who are absent for a day or for longer periods of time during the school year. Their duties include taking attendance, explaining homework, and maintaining classroom cleanliness.

NOTES

Many teachers have shared stories of being burn out, overworked, and fed up with low pay and the lack of respect. So many have stated that they are ready to quit.

NOTES

NEA is a national teacher's organization which has a wealth of information to keep parents informed. In a recent article in a recent Education Week survey, more than 75 percent of school principals and district leaders in the United States have reported challenges in hiring and keeping substitute teachers.

NOTES

You can research to see if your child's school is accredited. Accreditation is the recognition from an accrediting agency that an institution maintains a certain level of educational standards. The Department of Education maintains a data- base which it only recognizes.

https://www.zippia.com/substitute-teacher-jobs/demographics

NOTES

NBC news did an article where some schools were asking parents to become substitute teachers. What, some parents can barely handle their own kids at home. Let's not even consider them working with 20-30 of those little darlings.

NOTES

IES/NCES (National Center for Education Statistics) will provide up to date information on substitute teachers nationwide.

https://nces.ed.gov/whatsnew/press_releases/3_3_2022.asp

<u>NOTES</u>

CALLING ALL SUBS

 Substitute Teachers In the US
1,277,998

 Average Age
41.9

 Gender
Male - 27% Female - 73%

 Race
White - 62.9% Hispanic or Latino - 15.2%

 Most Common Degree

Bachelors - 67% Associate - 13%

Melvilyn Scott

There are certain words we should always try to have on our minds when working with students and supporting teachers. *Communication, encouragement, support, appreciation, patience,* we should *care,* have *consistency, unconditional love, discipline* because we love our children and show *concern* for our students and teachers.

†Hint... All the words being used are in italics.

CALLING ALL SUBS

DOWN

1. It is what everyone needs is _____
2. A TWO PHRASE WORD WE SHOULD ALL USE
3. How we show our stability is by being

    _____
4. Is what we should show to everyone that we

    _____

ACROSS

1. What we should have good lines of

    _____
2. We should all provide our children with

    _____
3. We should all show our children

    _____
4. We should show our teachers and children their
    _____ for all of their hard work
5. Our positive actions show that we have a

    _____
6. We a want to always provide _____.

Melvilyn Scott

According to Wester's Dictionary

1. *Appreciation*- *(noun)*
recognition and enjoyment of the good qualities of someone or something
We want to appreciate what our children are doing and their teachers.

2. *Care*- *(noun)*
the provision of what is necessary for the health, welfare, maintenance, and protection of someone or something.
We want to make sure that our children and their teachers know we care!

3. *Concern*- *(verb)*
relate to; be about.
We want to be able to relate to our children and their teachers.

4. *Communication*- *(noun)*
the imparting or exchanging of information or news.
We want to always have good lines of communication.

5. *Consistency*- *(noun)*
conformity in the application of something, typically that which is necessary for the sake of logic, accuracy, or fairness.
We want to provide consistency for our children to help establish rules and routines.

6. *Discipline*- *(noun)*
the practice of training people to obey rules or a code of behavior, using punishment to correct disobedience.
We want to discipline our children because we love them.

7. *Encouragement*- *(noun)*
the action of giving someone support, confidence, or hope.
We want to provide encouragement to our children and those who help our children.

8.Patience-*(noun)*
the capacity to accept or tolerate delay, trouble, or suffering without getting angry or upset.
We want to have patience with our students, their work and what is being required of them.

9.Support-*(verb)*
bear all or part of the weight of; hold up.
We want to support all of the positive endeavors for our students, faculty, teachers, staff, and administrators.

10.Unconditional Love-*(adjective)*
not subject to any conditions
We are going to love our children unconditionally.

About The Author

Melvilyn Scott is a proud wife of a loving and dedicated husband, three amazing adult children, two beautiful granddaughters, and one very special handsome great grandson. Mrs. Scott's children all attended public schools and she was an assertive and intrusive parent to ensure her children could obtain the best education possible. Mrs. Scott has worked in Human Services Field for over 30 years and is an educator with a passion for helping people.

Being led by God, Mrs. Scott started a consulting business named **HISWAY Consulting Services** which is an acronym for Helping People Succeed Within a Year. Some plant, some water, however, God will definitely give the increase!

CALLING ALL SUBS

Crossword Puzzle

		U											
		N											
		C	O	M	M	U	N	I	C	A	T	I	O	N
		O											
S		N											
U		D	I	S	C	P	L	I	N	E			
P		T											
P	A	I	T	E	N	C	E						
O		O											
R		N											
T		A	P	P	R	E	C	I	A	T	I	O	N
		L											
		L											
	C	O	N	C	E	R	N				C		
		V									O		
		E	N	C	O	U	R	A	G	E	M	E	N	T
			A								S		
			R								I		
			E								S		
											T		
											E		
											N		
											C		
											Y		

68

Melvilyn Scott

For those of you who would like to participate in the next book by adding one of your heartwarming stories please email me at:

Callingallsubsatthenextlevel@gmail.com to submit your story.
The Chapters will be:

1. This is My Journey…Let's Travel Together
2. So You Want to be a Substitute Teacher?
3. I Have Applied. Hire Me. Train Me. I Can Do This.
4. My First Day
5. Hazard Pay
6. Lunch?? What is That?
7. Resource and Recess
8. Dismissal-End of the Day…Now What?

This is not just for substitutes but also teachers
who have had experiences with substitute teachers!

CALLING ALL SUBS

Lined pages are included at the back of book for you to write your comments and thoughts about the book.
Then pass it on to a parent whose child is about to go to school for the first time...or better yet, give it to a teacher and let he or she know how much you appreciate them.

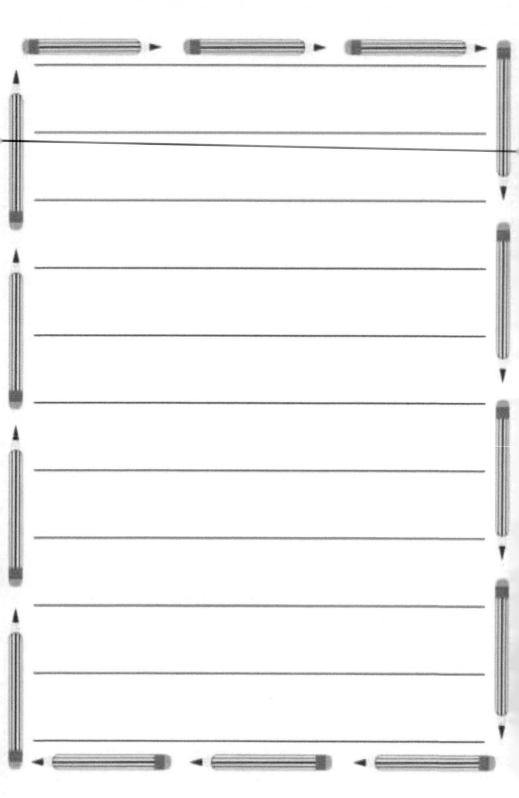

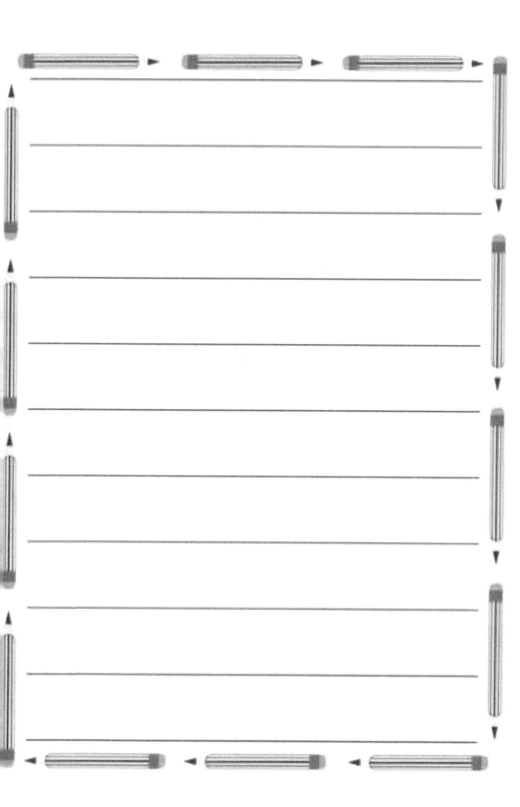

Melvilyn Scott

For more information, please email:
Callingallsubsatthenextlevel@gmail.com

Made in the USA
Columbia, SC
23 October 2022

69916921R00050